THE ILLUSTRATED WORLD OF
THE
VICTORIANS

Richard and Sara Wood

illustrated by
Adam Hook

HODDER
Wayland

an imprint of Hodder Children's Books

Also available:
The Illustrated World of the Tudors

© Copyright 2000 Hodder Wayland

Published in Great Britain in 2001 by Hodder Wayland,
an imprint of Hodder Children's Books
Reprinted in 2003
Editor: Philippa Smith
Designer: Sharon Huyshe

A Catalogue record for this book is available from
the British Library.

ISBN 0 7502 2616 1

Printed and bound in Hong Kong

Hodder Children's Books
A division of Hodder Headline Limited
338 Euston Road, London NW1 3BH

Contents

Words that appear in **bold** in the text are
explained in the glossary on page 30.

Victorian Times

 Victoria was the name of the Queen who ruled Britain from 1837 to 1901. We call the people who lived at this time the Victorians.

There are still many Victorian buildings in our towns and cities today, but almost everything else is different. Look carefully at this Victorian street scene. Count how many people were buying and selling goods on the street.

Life was very different for poor people. Their homes were often filthy and overcrowded, with large families crammed into just one or two rooms. They cooked over the sitting room fire – if they could afford to buy coal.

Most Victorians had no flush toilets. If they had a bath, they filled it from a jug or a single cold tap.

▼ *This poor girl was lucky. At least she had a bed to herself!*

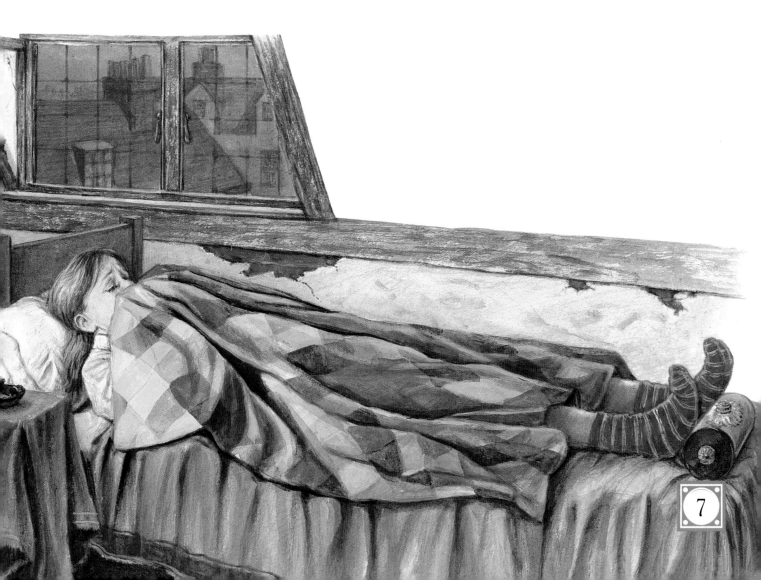

In Service

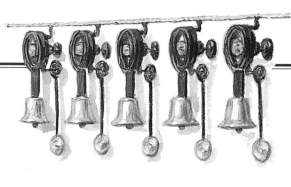

 The Victorians had no modern electric heaters, vacuum cleaners or washing machines. Instead, better-off families paid maids to do the housework for them.

Maids came from poor families and 'went into service' when they were about fourteen. It was often a hard, lonely life, in a strange house far from home.

▲ *The servants' bells rang to call the maid from the kitchen to a room in the house.*

◄ *A maid polishes the dinner gong.*

▼ *There was no inside toilet, so the maid had to empty the bedroom potties.*

In 1881, there were 2.5 million servants in Britain. Most worked in houses which employed just one maid.

Work started at 6 am, with fires to light. Later there were meals to cook and serve, rooms to clean and clothes to wash and mend. By 10 pm, when work ended, the maid was tired out.

▶ *Rich families sometimes had men servants, like this gardener.*

Victorian Food

◀ A baker takes loaves from the oven with a long-handled tool called a peel.

 Poor Victorian families often went hungry. Their meals were mainly of bread, potatoes or thin soup. Meat was a luxury they could only afford once or twice a week.

▲ Poor families often bought cheap meals from street sellers, like this baked-potato man.

▶ *The maid frying* **kippers**, *a popular Victorian breakfast dish.*

Richer homes usually had a coal-burning stove called a range. A cook might spend hours preparing a large dinner with many courses. There would be soup, fish, meat, vegetables, puddings and cheese.

▶ *A kitchen range, with its blazing fire, hotplate and ovens.*

Victorian Clothes

Which Victorians on this page were rich and which were poor? You can guess from the look of their clothes.

Poor people's clothes were often quite worn or ragged. Perhaps they were second-hand cast-offs from richer people. They did not expect to be smart or fashionable. They just tried to keep warm.

▼ *The poor street seller wears several thick layers of clothes to keep warm.*

◀ *Victorian men and women, poor as well as rich, almost always wore hats.*

Victorian Homes

This page shows the comfortable home of a well-off Victorian family. Large town houses like this had rooms on several floors. There was no electricity, so most rooms were heated by coal fires. At night, people lit candles and oil or gas lamps.

▲ *The grandfather clock was wound up once a week.*

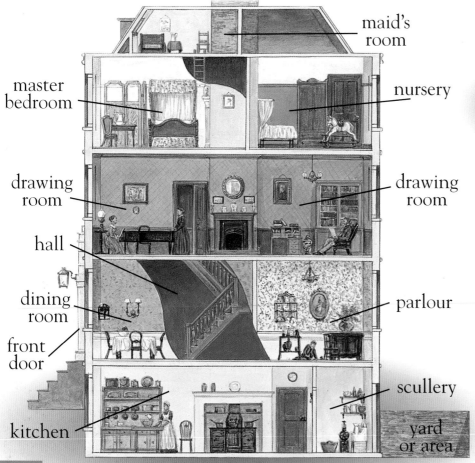

maid's room

master bedroom

nursery

drawing room

drawing room

hall

dining room

parlour

front door

kitchen

scullery

yard or area

◄ *A cutaway showing the rooms of a Victorian house.*

Victorian ladies' crinolines could be a danger at home. If they stood too close to the fire, they might go up in flames.

Rich Victorians kept up with changing fashions. For men, this meant silk top hats in the latest style. Ladies wore corsets to squeeze their waists. To make their dresses fan out, they wore wire cages underneath, called crinolines.

▶ *This rich lady's dress and hat were hand-made and very expensive. The street sweeper was too poor to buy himself shoes.*

Growing Up

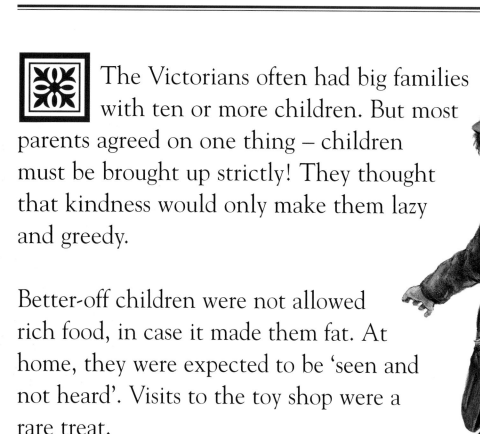

The Victorians often had big families with ten or more children. But most parents agreed on one thing – children must be brought up strictly! They thought that kindness would only make them lazy and greedy.

Better-off children were not allowed rich food, in case it made them fat. At home, they were expected to be 'seen and not heard'. Visits to the toy shop were a rare treat.

Poor children had very little time for play. They were sent out to work as soon as they were able. Their **wages** were needed to feed the family.

▲ *Poor children had few toys, so they played free games like hopscotch.*

▼ Most toys were hand-made and expensive. Only rich families could afford them.

Going to School

This picture shows one corner of a large Victorian schoolroom. See how many differences you can spot between your classroom and this one.

For literacy, the whole class read together, or copied words from the blackboard on to slates. Older children had ink pens and copybooks.

Until 1880, children did not have to go to school. Even then, they were allowed to leave as soon as they were ten.

Victorian schools were very strict. Anyone who made a mistake had to stand by the wall wearing the **dunce's hat**. Bad behaviour was punished by a hit on the hand with the cane.

Life in the Country

Until the 1850s, more people lived in the country than in towns. Most crops were still sown, weeded and harvested by hand. There were many animals to look after, too. At harvest time there was lots to do, so whole families joined in, earning extra money to buy new clothes and shoes.

Country families often kept a pig which they fed on scraps. To kill it, they slit its throat and collected the blood to make black puddings.

◀ *For poor people, life in a country cottage could be cold and lonely.*

▲ *This horse-drawn* **reaping** *machine replaced a gang of men with* **scythes**.

Later on, machines took over more and more farm work. Many people lost their jobs and moved away to towns to find work.

Better-off country people, like the **squire**, the farmer, the doctor and the vicar, usually had a very comfortable life. They had large houses, servants, and gardens where they grew their own fresh food.

19

Factories

Coal, cloth, pottery, iron goods, steam engines – these were some of the products that made Victorian Britain 'the workshop of the world'. New mills and factories opened. Small towns like Manchester and Leeds grew into huge cities. By late Victorian times, Britain was the world's richest country.

In early Victorian times, some children had to work over twelve hours a day, six days a week. After 1847, their hours were cut to no more than ten.

WARNING
CLIMBING OVER MULE HEADSTOCKS
IS STRICTLY PROHIBITED
THE MANAGEMENT WILL TAKE EXCEPTION TO
ANY CLAIM FOR COMPENSATION FOR
ARISING FROM THIS IRREGUL

But while some people grew rich, others were forced to work very long hours for low wages. Conditions in the factories and mines were often unhealthy and dangerous. Many poor people died in accidents.

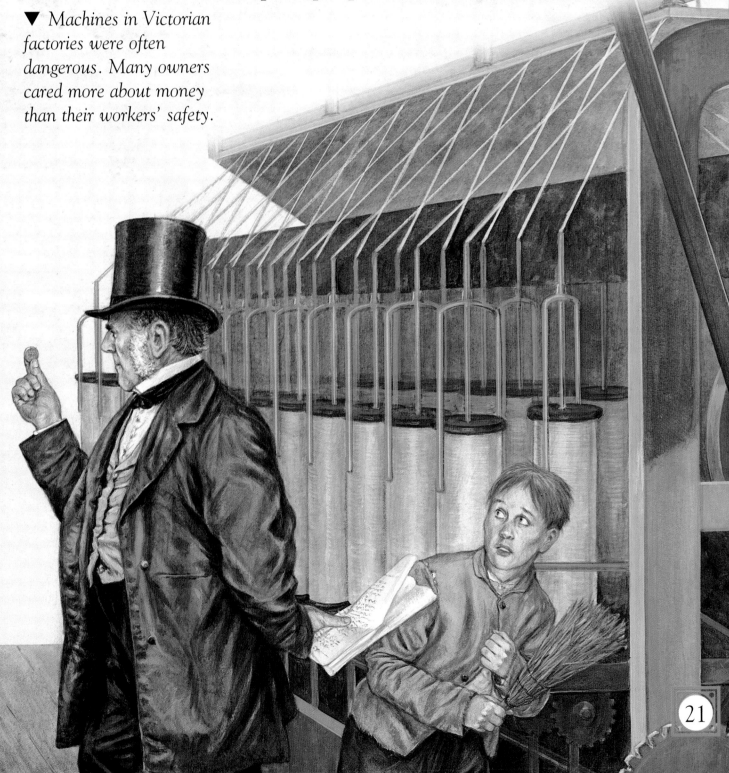

▼ *Machines in Victorian factories were often dangerous. Many owners cared more about money than their workers' safety.*

The Workhouse

The poorest Victorians lived in huge workhouses. Workhouse 'inmates', as they were called, had to earn their keep. They grew some of their own food and did simple jobs like breaking stones or unpicking old ropes.

▼ *Old women eating gruel, a sort of thin porridge. Gruel was often served for dinner in the workhouse.*

Charles Dickens' book *Oliver Twist* was about a boy brought up in a Victorian workhouse. It showed people how terrible the conditions were in some workhouses.

Most workhouse inmates were **widows** and old people, or children, some of them **orphans**. Life for them was hard. Men and women, boys and girls were kept apart.

Children over seven could only see their parents once a week. But at least they had food, a roof over their heads and warm clothing to wear.

▼ *The workhouse master shows a new inmate the rules of the workhouse.*

Having Fun

There were no video games or televisions in Victorian times. People had to make their own fun.

Most better-off people had pianos at home. Children learned to play music and sing, to entertain their families in the evenings. They also played games like tennis and **croquet**, or went on trips to the theatre.

▲ *A performance of Cinderella in a toy theatre.*

Perhaps you borrowed this book from a library. After 1850, many towns set up free libraries so that poorer people could read books.

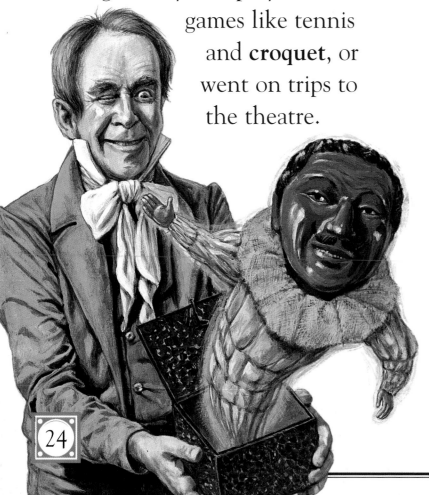

◀ *The jack-in-a-box man was a popular children's entertainer.*

▶ The **barrel organ** man and his dancing monkey often performed on the streets.

Poor Victorian children bought their 'footballs' from the butcher's shop. They could blow up a pig's **bladder** like a balloon, to kick in the streets.

Sometimes there was free entertainment in the streets from clowns, musicians or performing animals.

▶ Toys with moving parts or clockwork motors became very popular in Victorian times.

Sickness

 Most children born in Britain today will live to be 80. But Victorian people usually died much younger. Doctors charged high **fees** and did not have our modern medicines.

Even in rich families, many babies died of illnesses that would easily be cured today.

Dirty conditions caused many deaths. In the 1840s, more than half the children born in Manchester died before they were five years old.

◄ *'Coughs and sneezes spread diseases.' Many Victorians died from colds and flu.*

▶ *Doctors gave school children regular health checks. They sent home anyone who was ill to stop the other children catching infections.*

In towns, the death rate was especially high among the poor. Streets were often filthy and full of rats. The drinking water from rivers and wells was **polluted**. Terrible diseases like cholera and typhoid spread rapidly and killed millions of people.

▶ *The undertaker arranged the burial of dead people. He was easy to spot from his solemn black clothes.*

Celebrations

Victorian life may have been hard, but it was often fun, too. There were parties for christenings, marriages and birthdays. People exchanged presents on St Valentine's Day, watched processions on **Empire Day**, and lit bonfires on Guy Fawkes' night.

Many of our Christmas customs, like crackers, cards and visits from Father Christmas, began in Victorian times.

▼ Christmas trees became popular after the Queen had one decorated for the royal children.

▲ *Queen Victoria arrives at St Paul's Cathedral, London, for her Diamond Jubilee celebration.*

Queen Victoria was only nineteen when she became Queen. By the time she died in 1901, she had reigned longer than any other British **monarch**.

Perhaps the biggest party was for Queen Victoria's Diamond Jubilee in 1897. Millions of people gathered in the streets to celebrate Victoria's sixty years on the throne. For most people, life had become richer, healthier and safer than ever before. Everyone sang 'God Save the Queen'!

Now you've seen what life was like in Victorian times, would you like to have lived then instead of now?

Glossary

barrel organ	A small organ played by turning a handle.
bladder	A balloon-shaped part of an animal's intestine.
croquet (*crow-kay*)	An outdoor game played with hoops, balls and mallets.
dunce's hat	A cone-shaped hat worn by a child that the teacher said was stupid.
Empire Day	A public holiday in Victorian times celebrated on or near 24 May (Queen Victoria's birthday).
fees	The money someone charges for doing a job.
kippers	Smoked herring fish.
monarch	A king or queen.
orphans	Children whose parents have both died.
polluted	Dirty and infected with disease.
reaping	Cutting farm crops like wheat, barley or oats.
scythes	Long-handled tools with curved blades for cutting grass or crops.
squire	A country gentleman who owned land.
wages	The money someone earns from doing a job.
widow	A woman whose husband has died.

Books to Read

Home and School (Life in Victorian Times) by Neil Morris (Belitha, 1999)
Victoria (Our Kings and Queens) by Margaret Stephen (Wayland, 1999)
Victorians by Rachel Wright (Franklin Watts, 1997)
The Victorians (History Starts Here) by John Malam (Wayland, 1999)
Victorian Times (What Families Were Like) by Fiona Reynoldson (Wayland, 1998)

Places to Visit

Cogges Manor Farm
Cogges, Witney, Oxfordshire OX8 6LA (tel: 01993-772602)
www.aboutbritain.com/CoggesManorFarmMuseum.htm
A Victorian farm and house with opportunities to dress up and take part in activities.

The People's Story
163 Canongate, Royal Mile, Edinburgh EH8 8DD (tel: 0131-5294057)
Tableaux of Victorian life.

Norfolk Rural Life Museum
Gressebhall, Dereham, Norfolk NR20 4DR (tel: 01362-860563)
www.norfolk.gov.uk/tourism/museums/nrlm.htm
A former workhouse with recreations of Victorian country life and a working farm.

North of England Open Air Museum
Beamish, County Durham DH9 0RG (tel: 0191-3704000)
www.beamish.org.uk/visitor-info.htm
Ordinary Victorian families at home and at work brought to life by costumed interpreters.

Quarry Bank Mill
Styal, Cheshire SK9 4LA (tel. 01625-527468)
www.quarrybankmill.org.uk
A working cotton mill which shows what life was really like in a Victorian factory.

Ulster Folk and Transport Museum
Cultra, Holywood, Co. Down BT18 0EW (tel. 01232-428428)
www.nidex.com/uftm/index.htm
Visit furnished cottages and farms and see demonstrations of Victorian crafts.

Index